SHATTERED

sflynn6734@Gmail.com

SHATTERED

THOUGHTS OF LOVE AND HEARTACHE

BY

SEAN FLYNN

Shattered

*These writings are dedicated to love and all
who have known its truth.*

For in true love all is grand.

I appreciate the ability to draw, mostly because I couldn't draw a stick figure no matter how hard I tried. I gave The poems to a young Pakistani Girl to see what images they conjured for her. Her name is Tumpa and I hope you enjoyed her art.

Introduction

Once upon a time, right?

Haven't we all hoped with full hearts that we would eventually find 'the one' true love that would make everything alright?

Many have found that true heart, and that journey must be incredibly beautiful.

Others think they find the right one, only to realize years later the pieces did not fit into the puzzle quite right. Then, things eventually break down and hearts part, going separate ways. That is indeed tragic.

Of course there is another subgroup. Those fortunate enough to have found another who's inner light, personality, beauty, passion, sense of humor, patience, independence, strength and intellect was an incredible match. Add to that chemistry, connection and desire for one another that is undeniable and a foundation for a lifelong relationship has been laid. However, circumstances, choices, timing or outside forces kept or pulled you apart? This is the unrequited love and a bitter pill to swallow for certain.

But there is one worse scenario. Maybe you actually found that special person and for a time you rode that titanic wave across the ocean together only to find you weren't going to get to the 'happily ever after' shoreline. The reason doesn't matter. The end result, however, can wreak havoc on one's heart and soul for a long while, sometimes - forever.

Forever…

That sounds like such an ominous word. For it encompasses both the best of possibilities and the worst of potential outcomes.

When you buy in completely, commit yourself to another and end up on the wrong side of a split, it can be devastating. Finding a reason, whatever that may be does not make it any easier to take.

The fact is you're left carrying around an incredible amount of emotion and feelings, with virtually no outlet. Well, that is, unless you want to just be a drain on all of you family and friends. But that's definitely not very endearing, haha.

My situation was of my own making. I believed there was actually a chance with someone who was already tethered, who intimated that she was available. In the end, I was not chosen, I lost. It remains a monumental event in my life.

How could she take me along for this unbelievable, unmistakable, incredible journey knowing she was never fully committing to me? I'm convinced that this was never her intention, there was just too much at stake.

Was I truly stupid? Was I just a big, dumb lug with a big soft heart? Perhaps, but I completely believed in her, in us and I was sure we would celebrate the rest of our time together.

Writing these thoughts during the course of our time together was a way to celebrate our new love and to reckon with the feelings within myself when things appeared bleak and when they rekindled. It's kind of a 'to the brink and back' storyline.

No, this is not a 'woe is me' or 'please feel sorry for me' gathering of rants.

You may read it and ask yourself, how does this sad sack carry on?

Well, I suppose I continue to hold out hope, hope that she'll reconcile her situation and not choose to live a life in a loveless relationship. Without hope we simply fade away. In life it's not so much what you can live with but what you cannot live without.

Why print this then? No, I'm not looking for pity. Conversely, as I gathered these writings in one place it occurred to me that perhaps someone else who is in a challenging place might find some sense of relief in the words, either knowing that they are not alone or in relating to the experience and allowing themselves to let go, even if just a little bit.

You see, true love never dies. The reality is one never 'gets over' the loss of a true love. If they did, it wasn't true.

On Wings of Love We Soared

The flavor of renew

I staggered whence I came upon her
My breath being drawn away
To supplicate my eager heart
Waged war against my brain

Desire coursed my vein as fire
Brought my blood to boil
Inhaling full her very essence
A weary soul recoiled

Breathed her scent so deeply
Suffused me to the through
Fought the while to hold her there
This flavor of renew

The First Time

Unyielding,
Radiant,
Glowing natural beauty,
Vibrant,
Full of life,
Electric smile
And a rare innocence,
I would later learn.

She was both siren and serene,
Predator and prey,
Victor and victim.

The ride was euphoric,
The passion intense,
The Closeness was immeasurable,

The highs were epic -

- and there were no lows.

Home

It was instantaneous.

And I will say this;

Until this encounter
I had never believed
In any sort of love at first sight
Mumbo jumbo,

But I've never
Been more moved by a woman
Than by her.

In her presence everything
Outside of us evaporated,
Disappeared.

I found myself
In the eye of the storm
As the rest of the world
Spiraled out of Control around me.

She brought peace with her.

She was safe.

She was home.

The Fragrance of her soul

A leg astride my body,
A hand upon my chest
Her tummy pressed against my own
On top of me she rest
Wild hair in frenzy
Disguised those sultry eyes
Smiled at me through tangled strands
As fingers traced my thighs
Arms wrapped tight around me
Limbs became entwined
Bodies mingled, driving heat
To love both hearts resigned
Felt her softly settle
Inhaled her to the whole
Was then I knew when I breathed in
The fragrance of her soul

Obsession

I'll never comprehend the ins and out's
Of how chemistry works,
How attraction's laws
Are applied or governed,
But I faced arraignment
And was convicted on the spot.

From the moment I saw her
My thoughts were locked in shackles.
I could think of nothing else,
Of no one else.

My heart was imprisoned
At the sound of her voice,
At the sense of her touch,
At the taste of her kiss.

My blood boiled in her presence,
My pulse raced
At the mere thought of her.

Obsession is too soft a word
For how she affected me,
How she struck me.

It was like being hit with a sledgehammer,
Having an anvil dropped on my head.

I was actually dizzy, woozy,

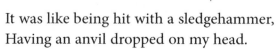

Shattered

But with the clarity of knowing
It could only be her,
It had to be her.

For the first time in my life
I realized that there were people
uniquely designed for each other.

I was for her what she was for me.

We were us
And we were
amazing together -

- When we Could be together.

The last spark

It takes a spark to light the fire,
Passions fuse to loves desire.
Awakened by an instant heat,
A burning want,
A need so deep

Was in her smile, a cogent snare,
In the deepest brown of eyes so rare.
The plea so quiet, yet deafening
'Imagine what tomorrow brings.'

The part of me that I thought dead,
Wrested from its lonely bed.
Pulled me out of deepest dark
The way was lit by my last spark

Virus Called Love

I loved that she was 100% girl,
Affectionate,
Attentive,
Seductively demure.

It was like a toxin
Coursing through my body,
Infecting me,
Collecting me.

She was the sickness I craved.
An attraction too strong to resist,
An addiction so compelling,
So desirable,
It couldn't be dismissed.

No pharmaceutical response
Could control it.

The truth is I didn't want to control it.

I wanted her disease,
I yearned for her special sickness,
I needed to be quarantined
In the infirmary of her sweet,
Viral love.

The Plunge

Okay, falling in love?
That was easy.
She was everything and everywhere all at once.

She dazzled me,
Delighted me,
Devoured and ignited me.

She teased me,
Excited me,
Tempted and incited me.

Her voice was intoxicating,
Her smile infectious
And her laugh Contagious.

She moved me as a pawn
All over her Chess Board
And after toying with me
Long enough to please her,
She easily had me 'mated'.

Game Over –

- Sometimes losing, is winning

Surrounded

Her love was immense and intense,
Enveloping and securing.
The soft sound of her quiet voice
In a Crazy world was reassuring.
Her Gentle way was Calming to an anxious man.

How could such a small package
Fill so much space,
In my mind,
In my heart
And surround me so completely,
With such unmatched sensitivity and beauty.

Even with all of her inner turmoil,
Her questions and contradictions.

Even in duplicity
She always found a way to focus on me,
On us,
When we were together.

I'm not certain if that was due to her love for me
Or if she was so lost
That she held onto anything that kept her anchored,
Even if only for awhile.

But the while she was with me
She surrounded me with love.

Sliced and Diced

She wielded love as a sword,
She sliced away at my bitterness and anger,
My self loathing,
Fear and trepidation with intimacy.

She carved away the chaff
And left me standing,
Weightless,
Boundless
And free to love again.

And I loved her fiercely
With a consuming, fiery passion
Unlike any
I had previously known.

forbidden fruit

The fruit that belongs to another,
As if any one of us belongs to another human,
Forbidden,
Taboo,
Is there something about it
That makes it more savory?

But to be sure:

If love had a taste,
It would be her.
It's in her kiss.

If love had a feel,
It would be her.
It's in her touch.

If love Could be seen,
It would be her.
It's in her eyes.

If love had aroma,
It would be her.
It's nestled in her very essence.

If love had a hue,
It would be her.
It's in the Color of her soft, sweet voice.

If love had a sound,
It would be her.
It's in the steady rhythm of her tender heartbeat.

I know,
As I have seen it, touched it and heard it.

For she gave me her love.

Blinded

I've never held a woman so tightly,
So closely,
So relentlessly.

I've never missed a girl so completely,
So dire,
So fiercely.

We were the easiest pieces
of the puzzle to connect.
Everything simply came together,
Just fell into place.

We were each,
Exactly what the other needed.

We couldn't stay away from one another,
Even when we tried.

I was the fly
And she the ointment.

I was the moth,
She, the flame,
So hot,
Intense was her heat,
Bright was her light...

...blinding.

Addicted and Afflicted

An itch to scratch,
disease unlatched,
light the fire,
strike the match,
a desperate need to satisfy,
desire cried,
burning,
gnawing,
deep inside
the melted spoon,
flame to metal,
heads in swoon,
heat ignites,
intensifies,
liquified,
drawn into love's syringe,
injected,
pain so sharp,
the pinch, a twinge,
she coursed through me,
racing through my body,
racing to my heart,
warming me,
caressing me,
sublime,
so high,
higher than a kite,
higher than a bird in flight,
so high we must keep out of sight,
invisible, yet indivisible.

Addicted to her recklessly,
afflicted by her chemistry.

Reflections

She held my heart
But I was never allowed to completely hold hers.
It was carefully guarded.
Though she could clearly see what I needed,
Her vision was a bit impaired
When she looked in the mirror.
She could not so easily see,
Or could not reckon with,
What it was she truly needed.

Need Me, Touch Me, Tell Me

Need Me,

Touch Me,

Tell Me.

Lips find lips, skin meets skin,
Hearts alight, Love excites,
Overflowing, Heat ignites
Rejuvenated, energized
As whispers on the wind
Encircling, embracing,
Every hair and nerve on end.
Ears of promise hear their want,
Smoldering fires beckon, taunt
Her smile teased, her tongue it pleased
Flirting, wanting, a heart in siege
Passions rise, love collides
Desires climb, reaching, stretching,
Straining –

Need Me

Touch Me

Tell Me

The air stood still and I sank into the abyss

Realizations

It's an unfortunate realization
That to best write about pain,
One must be in pain.

Never Yours

Let it go,
it was never yours.
You held it for awhile,
for a time it laid against your own,
pressed so close,
like nothing you had ever known
You felt the rhythm of it's beat,
the burning of it's heat,
now the taste so bittersweet.

Let it go,
it was never yours.
Calloused our own hearts become,
besieged in pain,
grown so numb.
Yet still we cling to what we know,
Despite the fear we keep in tow.

Why is it you hear the sound,
that beats so loud,
without you now?

Was something there?
You'll never know,
was never yours,

so
let
it
go

Precariously perilous

Love is so precariously perilous -

I realized when I gave mine to her,
When I crossed that line
and completely bought in,
that I had also given her
the ability
to destroy me.

How sweet the destruction.

I just need to Figure out what to do
with all the rubble –

Love's lies

Love lies waiting in hungry eyes,
in lonely hearts that's where it hides.
Love lies waiting in hates' despise,
in spurned emotion it wears disguise.
Love lies waiting in Hope and chance,
an open door, in circumstance.
Love lies waiting in empty beds,
In touch unfed and words unsaid.
Love lies waiting in temptation,
dissatisfaction, aggravation.
Love lies waiting in many places,
few dispute the count of spaces.
Love lies waiting everywhere,
waits for you if you dare.
Love lies waiting if you decide
to take the risk, enjoy the ride.
Just bear in mind the other side
when you test the lips that tell love's lies.

...Missed

The way she looked through ardent eyes,
that melted at my soul,
the secret of her misery,
her tenderness in whole.

The dream of mingled futures,
the promise of 'someday',
the very possibility,
in every new born day.

Her gentle conversation,
the passion in her pain,
the raw anticipation,
of holding her again.

The cadence of her heartbeat,
the chance in each tomorrow,
and any opportunity,
to take away her sorrow.

Each solitary smile,
the taste of every kiss,
the lingering of her frailty,
the softness of her lips.

Took only just a moment.
to draft this tiny list,
the empty way I feel inside,
Confessing things I miss.

Comes down to choice

Comes down to choice
the things we choose,
who we keep, who we lose.

Comes down to choice
the things we want,
what's important and what is not.

Comes down to choice
the things we need,
the things we hold or just set free.

Comes down to choice
the seeds we sow,
what we embrace, what we let go.

Regret and sorrow still the voice,
when we neglect to make the choice.

There, Somewhere, Anywhere

There, somewhere, anywhere,
vast unswerving dubiety,
no escape,
no solitude,
ruminations dominate the helpless,
the hopeless,
the elusiveness of understanding is torment,
unpack it -

- no,
pack it,
store it,
lock it away,
give it no mind,
no time,
runaway,
hide,

there,
somewhere,
anywhere.

Lost

It's so very odd how we say
we 'found' the one.

Even more ironic
how someone who you once counted on,
who you were pointed to like a compass,
who helped provide you with direction
and kept you steady,
can also be the one person
to completely derail you
and leave thrown off track,
wondering hopelessly,
wandering aimlessely through life
both physically and emotionally -

- lost.

The Unexpected Gardener

It was her who cultivated the seed of love,
she planted it,
she watered it,
she fed it,
she grew the love
with her own incredible,
amazing, wonderfulness

It may not have been intentional
but there was no stopping it,
once it had been planted.

Eventually,
she was lured into
the garden she had created.
I don't think she ever expected
she could be trapped there
but she was.

It was so safe there,
She made me her safe place.

Comfortable,
warm
and inviting.

When the time came
to reap the love that she had sown,
she could not.

There were other flowers to tend to
and the Harvest rewards
Just didn't add up
in the new garden.

It's not that I lost,
for I Believe,
we both lost.

A Particular Girl

Was she afraid of me
Or afraid of herself?

Afraid to be free,
Or afraid we would fail

The proverbial question looms
For love, or money

Ocean of Emotion

Even after all of our time together
she remains an unsolvable riddle,
a contradiction and confliction,
a great unknown

She was an ocean of emotion
a mountain of love
a treasure trove of knowledge
Yet a carefully guarded soul

It took time to understand that
because she was so very good at being present
when we shared company.

...My Pain

No one wants to hear my pain.
They have pain of their own.

Maybe if I write it down
they might read it
and some of the sting will go away?

Maybe if I sing it out loud,
really loud,
someone will hear it
and take some of it from me?

No,
I don't want to hurt anyone
with my pain,
I just want it to go away.

Surely she must've taken
some of it with her?

I did not want that.
I was supposed to take hers away.

Maybe I did?
Maybe this is hers.
In that case
That would be okay.
I will embrace the pain.

Completely Incomplete

You can't erase a hole.
You can patch it,
Cover it up,
You can paint over it,
try to hide it,
But the hole is still there

The place where the hole is
has become compromised,
it is weaker.

The structure
where the hole was made
is no longer stable.

The only way to get rid of the hole
is to rebuild the entire structure.

When she left,
she made a hole.
And it's a big hole.
Now I'm completely, Incomplete.

Unfortunately you can't rebuild
a human heart.

Just to breathe

The struggle to breathe,
won't concede,
just to breathe.

I can't shake the thoughts that plague me,
they invade me,
drive me crazy.

Can't break the chains that bind me,
deep inside me,
they can blind me.

Taking away things that I need,
the air that I breathe.

I Can't scale the walls that pain me,
they contain me,
so constrain me,

Can't chase the fears that scare me,
they impair me,
break and tear me down,
taking away the things that I need,
the air that I breathe.

Insanely afflicted,
a heart so constricted,
no matter how hard I try,
emptiness deep inside,
just doesn't concede,
won't recede.

I struggle to breathe,
Just to breathe.

40   *Shattered*

A Blessing Or A Curse

The reason I hurt so badly
Is that I chanced to love so deeply

Burned

Make the most of every moment,
take advantage of every opportunity.
Give relentlessly,
love recklessely
but never expect that will be enough.

The hint of happiness
is but a spark
and sometimes,
even if you are able
to whip it into a
full fledged wildfire
you may still lose what you sought.

You may still end up -

- burned!

Living In Limbo

My address?
1N limbo
Constantly, USA

This is a crappy neighborhood

A place where some decisions are never made,
plans fall through
and actions rarely match the words that are spoken

What next

Unsettled,
restless,
uncertain steps call me forward,
don't look back,
so ugly,
let it burn,
let the smoke carry it away on the wind,
until dissipated, the sky is clear.

Rain comes,
crashing down,
odious droplets pelt recklessly
from angry clouds,
gathering,
pooling,
trickles carrying burnt remnants
of the past,
flowing like a river at my feet.

Can't cross it,
can't turn back,

Unsettled,
restless,
uncertain steps.

Shattered

Grand the beauty

As flashing lightning in the sky
her brightness overtook my eyes.
It danced and dazzled, teasing, free,
taunting, calling, haunting, please

Intense, exploding through the shroud,
a painted cry among the cloud.
So grand the beauty storms can bring,
She wore it lie her angel wings.

Washed away my deepest stain,
pure, desire, healed the pain.
The storm it raged on deep inside,
heart or mind, the great divide.

To leap, to chance, could she decide?
An unknown path, a changing tide
But lightning comes sporadically,
so grand the beauty storms can bring.

Where goes that beauty in-between?

Where once I flew

Where once I flew on broken wings
Wind that lifted, only stings
Empty, listless, called my name,
washed away a dirty stain
soared so high I failed to see
the road ahead, catastrophe
Hold on, I reached,
grasped only air
Strained, desired, nothing there
We touched, awhile, a moment, gone
Confused, emotions, linger on
Drifting, stuck, remembering,
Where once I knew, awakenings,

Where once I flew on broken wings.

In another's hand

A scary thing to understand
that your heart is held in another's hand
more frightening still when it's returned
in shattered pieces, your love spurned

A Glimpse

Caught a glimpse of beauty
uncommon, out of place
a rose amongst the thornbush
conflicted in that space

Caught a glimpse of beauty
atop the slender stem
soft and supple to the touch
grace and elegance in blend

Caught a glimpse of beauty
nestled in the shade
With comely petals opened
Come dance with me she played

Caught a glimpse of beauty
radiantly rare
gilded by privation
instantly ensnared

Caught a glimpse of beauty
stunningly unique
trapped beyond the garden rail
draped in grand mystique

Caught a glimpse of beauty
that couldn't be plucked out
secure in her surroundings
hidden in her doubt

Caught a glimpse of beauty
not if by happenstance
tried in best, love will attest
I just wasn't worth the chance

If

If I'm important to you
then treat me like I'm important
make a place for me,
text me, call me, reach me,
be there, find a way, somehow –
Why?
You give your time to things that are important

If I'm valuable to you
then tell me I'm worth it
tell me how you feel
It should be in your eyes, in your voice,
in your touch and in your commitment –
Why?
You give attention to things you value

If you love me
don't just tell me,
show me
make me believe with the things you do
move me with your kisses
envelop me in your nearness
absorb me into your soul –
Why?
You give your heart and yourself to what you love

If I really matter to you
then your actions
should match your words

Shattered

be authentic, be consistent,
do what your heart tells you to do,
be truthful, sincere and genuine,
even if it hurts

who feels important who is ignored?
who feels valuable who is alone?
who feels loved who is wondering?

who is you?

who is me?

who and what are we?

Away His Heart

With abandon it was reckless
how he gave away his heart
without retreat, he gave complete
He knew right from the start
Based solely on a promise
of a love uncompromised
she laid the bait, that he thought fate
tripped up by love's disguise

There love lies

On a bed of roses, there love lies,
innocence imposes, fingers, hands and tongues, entwined,
passion, fire, hearts resigned.
Loves freeing promise,
sparks ignite,
intense, illuminating,
only light,
burning, sizzling,
nova bright,
raw, exploding,
love takes flight.
Racing to the highest height,
soaring,
weightless through the sky.

A sudden change,
a fall not slow,
soon appeared the doom below.
Feelings, questions raining down,
rushing, crashing, to the ground,
pieces scattered everywhere,
remnants of a hearts despair.

He scratched and crawled,
so compromised,
he stared into those empty eyes,
no answers, reasons or alibis,
no one last kiss,
no sweet goodbye's,
words once tempted,

Shattered

lips confide,
unknown secrets always hide.

It's only when she speaks he cried,
I know it now,
there love lies.

Out of Love

I never stopped loving her.
Falling out of love Just didn't happen for me.
It was more like being pushed from an airplane at 30,000 feet -
- Without a parachute.

And I'm so dense
that every cloud I passed
on the way down
was another memory
of how good we were together,
how much we enjoyed each other,
how much love we shared,
how much fun we had,
how much I didn't want it to end,
how much...

SPLAT!

Drops of the Heart

Love,
A healing elixir and a poison,
simultaneously.

It tastes so good going down
and knowing it is temporary on this earth,
even as we drink of it
we understand
that in the end love's sweet poison
will most likely destroy us
from the inside out.

Its destructive footprint
will render us hopeless
and helpless for a time.

Some will rebuild,
some will reload
and some will quit,
never again to be humiliated
by one whose actions
do not match their words.

Never again
to have their heart pared
like fruit
and splayed open
to bleed
until the laughing maggots of indignance
overtake it,
feasting in wait
for the next victim.

In Favor of Another's Heart

Someone once told me love is war.

War against what?
Apathy and not allowing feelings to dim?
War against misunderstanding
Fought with bullets of communication?
War against self in favor of another's heart?

Why is love war?

There should be no fight in love,
no struggle for power or position.
Only the desire
to make each other happy,
to build and nurture,
motivate and sustain.

We lose the war
when we lose the desire
to protect what we have,
when we stop favoring
another's heart over our own.

When a military war ends
the world rejoices,
the battle is over,
the suffering is ending.

When a love affair ends
pain and suffering are Just beginning.

Who wants to wage that war?

Win the battle first,
favor your others heart
over your own.

She Took The Light

Cold,

Empty,

Alone.

In this place where I rest
it's hard to tell which is worse.
Yet here there is some odd sense of comfort,
Some strange kind of foreboding peace,
A blankness,
A numbness,
Resonating through the chambers of my heart,
My soul.
The exhausting acceptance of futility.
No more expectations,
No hope in the future.

It's easy to fall.
Was drawn by promise,
Lured by her light,

But like a thief she took all,
Under cover of darkness and absconded,
Depositing what was left of me,
In broken, tired pieces,
Huddled in this expansive emptiness

Yes, she put me here,
But it was my blindness that allowed it.
Now even with open eyes
I still can't find the way out,
She took the light

But that's okay,
In her confused state of confliction,
Her dark and doubtful world,
She needs it more than me

Hopefully she'll use that light
to find herself,
to find her way,
to find her happy
to find the love her soul Craves.

For that would make my darkness
worth every second.

Shattered

Aches

Desire, Need, Want.

At first I ached to be with her,
near her,
in her regenerative,
nurturing company.
She was like a power outlet,
I could just connect to her
and I was recharged and rejuvenated.
My love meter filled to the brink,
my heart warm and my head clear.

Then I ached for her,
for her emptiness,
for her pain,
for what she could not see,
for where she was headed,
for her tragedy.
Was I draining her,
pulling her down,
making things more difficult?

Then I ached because of her,
her Choices,
her faulty reasoning,
her lack of faith in me,
Judging me
as if I was not good enough for her,
I didn't have my 'shit' together.
The ache became so big
it washed over me,
began to drown me
yet I still ached to swim with her,
and I still want to swim with her.

The Gentle Wind

The gentle wind it whispered
as it swept across my face
first kissing me, then lifting me
to a warmer, safer place

The gentle wind it whistled
as it passed aside my frame
caressingly, it said to me
'you'll never be the same'

The gentle wind it gusted
as it whisked away the pain
the dust it smeared, the fog it cleared
so I could see again

The gentle wind it howled
as I held it in my hand
it swirled around, free, unbound
teasing 'catch me if you can'

The gentle wind subsided
gave way to freezing rain
now just a breeze, each droplet stings,

so quiet -

alone -

again!

Ever on I sail

Ever on I sail,
Through the open, boundless sea,
Though she's gone away,
the wind who carried me.
Though the current runs
with the changing tide,
It has come and gone,
adrift inside

Ever on I sail,
Under empty, cloudless skies,
Though she's gone away,
the light who filled my eyes.
Though the bright of sun
shares its' warmth all day,
It has come undone,
I've lost my way

Ever on I sail,
No safe harbor lay in sight,
Though the future looms,
like the dark of night.
Though the stars still shine
and the winds may wail,
With no port in sight,
ever on I sail

Swept Away

It burst upon the open ground
A thrash of torrents raining down
The force of which without delay
wrest the heart, just swept away

It showered with exciting sound
loudly splashing, hearts would pound
The cleansing drum of liquid play
beats the heart, just swept away

It poured onto the desert sand
the quiet droplets kissed the land
the gentle lure of summer rain
warmed the heart, just swept away

It crashed with thunder, striking, loud
a tidal wave within the cloud
then just as quickly as it came
drowned the heart, just swept away

A drizzle, mist all that remains
Broke the heart,
just swept away

Shattered

...To Dance?

Why do I crave to spend time
With one who cannot make time for me?
Why do I ache for the touch
Of one who is constantly out of reach?
Why do my eyes strain to see
One who is mostly out of sight?
Why am I desperately reaching
For one so far away?
Why is it that I wish to dance so badly
With one who doesn't care to dance with me?

Even Now

Why?
Why did the dance end?
The music kept on playing,
the band roared on.
I reached for you but you disappeared,
slipped away in the crowd,
still wonder how it happened,
how it happened, even now.

Why?
Why did the conversation stop?
The topics never dwindled,
our voices weren't gone.
I called to you but you didn't hear
or wasn't clear, the sound,
still wonder how it happened,
how it happened,
even now.

Why?
Why did the party rear?
Champagne yet bubbled in the glasses,
the people mingled on.
searched everywhere to find you, y
ou were nowhere to be found,
still wonder how it happened,
how it happened,
even now.

Humble Crumble

I'm humbled when I do recall
how much to me she gave
But crumble when I realize
how much of me she took away

Into the deep

His was a large, old, yet confident seaworthy craft. After many years of service, it sailed aimlessly in new waters, enjoying the change of scenery, relaxing under the broad sail of release, taking in the sunshine and air fresher than it could remember.

One day the old boat sailed into a new harbor. If a boat could, it blushed at the beauty of the majestic ship moored at the center of the marina. He gazed upon the boat with covetous eyes wishing that someday he might sail with her.

Surprisingly, the beautiful ship was a bit captivated by the grace and confidence of the old boat. Despite the obvious superficial flaws in the aged slew he continued to circle the gorgeous ship day after day, getting her attention, hoping to coax her into sailing with him.

Their game of circling and bobbing on the wavelets, dancing together in the harbor was more fun than either could remember. They became so close that neither of the boats felt the same without the other.

There was much promise of trips they would share in exotic waters and the old boat longed to sail away into the sunset with the majestic, beautiful ship.

It wasn't that the pretty ship didn't want to sail again but it was moored in the harbor and could only sail occasionally, when the tide permitted. Besides, it was torn between the old boat and the comfort and familiarity of the harbor in which she rest.

The old boat fianally realized that the mooring was stronger than the beautiful ship had portrayed and reluctantly left the harbor, sadder than it had ever been.

Soon after it left the marina and the mesmerizing ship behind, the bilge pump began to fail and the old boat took on water. Without the hope of ever sailing those distant seas together the old boat listed, eventually slipping into the deep.

Between Us

My love for you
Is wider than the Grand Canyon,
I told her.

I love you
To the moon and back,
I said.

This love is deeper
Than the bottomless sea,
I promised.

Love like this
Outlasts the sands of time,
I plead.

Ironic that all I feel now
Is the distance between us.

The Game

The princess and the pauper

The lady and the tramp

In the game of love or money

I was way out of my class

A purse that knows no limit

Or the heart that knows romance

In the game of love or money

I never stood a chance

Summer Heat

Autumn took the skies today
The heat of summer waned
Leaves began to turn away
A weary heart complained
The cooling wind remembered
And darkness eyed the fall
Promises we'd rendered
Now just a distant call

I watched a feather dance the wind
Drifting on its ride
An aimless game which underpinned
The emptiness inside
A sudden blast of sunlight
Pierced the winters' freeze
Reluctantly the day bright
Gave way to stormy seas

The thaw came and uncovered
The birth of something new
Was then that I discovered
I had no chance in you
Spring had found the air again
With lovers everywhere
Secluded by an ailing heart
Befriended by despair

Seasons Turn

The earth is Just more lovely
Under freshly fallen snow
The heart at its most bountiful
When new love starts to Grow
A smile glows most radiant
As passions fire burns
Everything so beautiful
Until the season turns

Half a Heart

Love;
How can that word even be said
Without complete conviction;
By one with only half a heart invested

Love means being all in,
Accepting,
Understanding,
Coming to the line,
Meeting half way.

Love means sharing,
In the pleasure and the pain,

So which is worse,
She who said it?
Or the idiot who believed it?

Empty

My hope hung
On your heart
It clung
To the thin skin
Of indecision

Seeds of Love

How could I have been expected
To water the seeds of love
If I'm rarely allowed
to sit in the garden
How could I fan the flame
Of a love
that burned
Only intermittently

When we were together
It raged so hot
That we melted into each other.
But it still wasn't enough

Where am I?

I still struggle
To see Where it was I fell
I thought I was in Heaven
But I may have missed it
What kind of place is it
Where I'm only important
When she wants to see me?

Swirling Winds Remind Me

Are your ears popping yet?

It seems to me
That you are either on the top of the mountain,
High on love,

Or on the slippery slope,
Headed toward eventual heartache.

There is no in between.

In between is stale,
Stagnant,
The first stages of dead.

The descent down the slope
Is murderous,
The air pressure squeezing your head,
Tumbling,
Grasping,
Hoping.

Still, eventually,
When you hit rock bottom
You'll rest awhile,
Take stock of the damage,
Gather yourself together
And like a mindless drone
Start the climb
Back up the mountain again.

Because the air is so crisp,
The air is so clean.
Into forever you think you see.
It feels so good on the top of the mountain.

What is the definition of insanity?
Doing the same thing over and over again
Expecting a different outcome.

Are your ears popping yet?

Perception

Changing

'How Could she not see what we had?'

to

'What had I done to Cloud her vision?'

was not an easy transition.

My Weakness...

...and what of strength.

I'm no weakling,
I'm as strong as anyone else my size,
I can bench 300lbs,
lift furniture,
move refrigerators.

But I'm not strong enough to resist her.

She's my drug
and that addiction runs so deep
I fear I'd walk off of a cliff
if I thought she was calling me there.

She's that compelling,
that desirable.

It's a haunting love,
a desperate need.

Is the brain a muscle?
If it is, mines atrophied,

it has no fight against her,
no resolve to keep me from my drug.

Here, There, Everywhere

Sailing is not sailing without the water.
It is drifting.

Flying is not flying without the air.
It is falling.

Running is not running without the Ground.
It is sinking.

She was my motion,
my Commotion,
my loves devotion.

She was like water, Ground and air to me.

Here, there, everywhere.

Alligator arms

I still awaken in the wee morning hours,
reaching for her,
trying to find her,
to pull her close and envelop her in my clutch.

I really wish my arms were longer.

Let's Get Wet

She opened me like a book
and the words spilled off of the pages.

I read to her of my past and my pain,
my trials who like rain,
fell fully,
drenching her,
saturating her with my openness,
vulnerability,
my transparency.

It was Cleansing-
and to be in the umbrella
of her love was
Comfortable,
home,
safe.

Yet even with that level of intimacy
she couldn't complete the connection.

I wonder now if that umbrella
was just meant to keep her
from getting wet?

Shattered

Those eyes

Eyes come in all types
but it doesn't matter the color or the shape,
it doesn't matter the size
or the position they occupy on the face
what matters about eyes
is what you see when you look into them

Are they reflective eyes,
giving you back
their image of you?

Are they inviting eyes,
with an honesty and openness
that makes them safe?

Are they mysterious eyes,
that tease and taunt
but still leave you guessing?

Are they whimsical eyes,
playful and full of happiness?

Hers were all of the above
and were always filled with love.

It breaks my heart to realize
I no longer gaze into those eyes

Rollercoaster

A flaming love that burned so bright
Lit my world in dazzling light
Soared with me in dizzy height
Abandoned in the dark of night

A flaming love, a heart on fire
Jacked me with intense desire
Together we flew higher, higher
Faded out, a love retired

A flaming love, a searing heat
Beckoned me with every beat
Words of love she won't repeat
Searching, empty, incomplete

Slipping away

The rain returned again today
and nudged me back to bed
Tried to sleep the pain away
but dreamt of you instead
each droplet brought a memory
a reminder trapped in time
locked inside the chambers
of my efficacious mind

Proudly, Proud

A award to one who did not appreciate the gift.
I came across that trophy
hidden and ignored
and took the time to carefully,
lovingly, polish it to a pristine shine,
its beauty unsurpassed.

Though I could not display it
I put it in a place of prominence,
in my heart,
in my life
and gazed upon it with contented eyes
as it found its blazing radiance
once again.

It is nothing short of a tragedy for me
that the trophy was more comfortable
tucked away in the back of a closet,
in the dark,
covered by Junk,
rather than in my hands,
glowing brightly.

In The 'Zone'

I no longer wonder what if feels like
to be wished into the cornfield –

Just Look Back?

The fear of the unknown.
It still torments and haunts me,
Challenges and taunts me.

It was a life lived in limbo,
in flux.
Never really knowing what could have been,
Or where it might have gone.

What we shared
was nothing short of amazing
on every level,
emotional, intellectual, physical.

Our connection was ridiculous,
our chemistry off the charts.

Even though she could only give so much,
could only gift me
with what she was capable of making time for.

Should I be mad at her for that?

No!

What she did give me
was cathartic,
reinforcing,
life changing,
sublime.

Maybe I should just look back and smile

Oh, but she was so much of that smile.

Shattered

LYF

Love
   You
      Forever...

...LYF

That's what I would tell her.

She brought forth from me
a part of my lyf
that had been in deep repose.

She remains...

...amazing.

Once, for all

Everyone should get to love,
With reckless abandon,
with boundless passion,
Intense attraction.

Everyone should know a love,
That took a chance,
Where hearts could dance,
In pure romance.

Everyone should share a love,
where souls are found,
Where joys abound,
with great resound.

At least once,
an all encompassing love
should be had by all.

If I hadn't met her
I'd never have known the depth of feeling
of which I was capable.

For that I'm grateful.

Words So Sweet

Sweet words are just that, sweet.

They may drip with and evince, love.

But it is actions that convict those words

and convince the heart.

A Cursed Verse

I wish I would have found her first
That it was me who made her hearts love burst
That deep in me she became immersed
And only I could quench her thirst
That all her fears I would disperse

My timing couldn't have been worse

Don't Let Go

If I'm looking back
On all that I've done
What kind of man would I say
I have become?
I'm not rich
I'm not wise
Most of my life I've lived empty
Hiding behind a disguise
But it's opened my eyes

If I'm keeping track
Of things I've amassed
How will I ever look forward
With eyes in the past?
I'm not strong
I'm broken inside
I wear the stains of a lifetime
Painted in my foolish pride
But it's opened my eyes

So, please don't let go
Hold onto me
'Cause I'm falling, I'm falling
I fell, so effortlessly
Don't let me go
'Cause I'm Calling
And when I cry out
I cry out
faithfully

Out

Cry it out,
scream it out,
sing it out,
write it out,
but get it out, all out.

Because stuffing it,
Burying it,
hiding it,
or ignoring it won't work.

It will literally kill you from the inside -

- Out

...Alive

Pain isn't necessarily all bad -
Besides, you can't hide from it.
If it's there,
then it's there.
Until you confront it,
at least it reminds you,
you are still...

...alive

Again

She offered me her fruit,
"How does it taste?" she asked.
"So sweet, like nectar,
pure, delicious." I answered.

She offered me her heart,
"How does it sound?" she laughed.
"Strong, steady, like a piston,
yet soft and harmonious."

She offered me her love,
"How does it feel?" she teased.
"Soothing, rejuvenating, regenerative
and with the warmth of the bright sun.

It blew over me like the summer breeze,
Calming me and calling me.

I keep listening to the wind,
every subtle whisper,
every gentle gust,
every wonderful whistle,
every heavenly howl –

- hoping to hear that beautiful call,

Again

Tender Gifts

The most lithe of arms,
Hugged me into peace.
The softest, sweetest lips,
Kissed me into bliss.
The purest, tender heart,
Loved me into euphoria.

I shall always remember that,
No matter how long I wander.

What will she remember?

The Depths

How important is depth of soul,
if there is no one swimming
with you in those waters?
If you sink there,
alone,
that very depth
may drown you.

The Void

Loneliness is not being alone
It is far worse
Loneliness implies
that the absence of something
or someone,
once so fulfilling,
left an emptiness so expansive
that even in being in the presence of others,
no matter the number,

Cannot be filled.

Sometimes...

Sometimes it just ends
Sometimes we don't know why
Sometimes we're left wondering
Sometimes we wail and cry

Sometimes we seek answers
Sometimes we'll never know
Sometimes we keep on hoping
Sometimes we just let go

Sometimes we're stuck in limbo
Sometimes things can change
Sometimes we're better left alone
Sometimes we love again

Sometimes we love again

Wish your eyes were mine

Wish your eyes were mine.
Through eyes so open how clearly could I see,
just what the world might truly be,
how I might look to someone else
despite the way I see myself,
the darkness safely filtered out,
where confidence replaces doubt,
the dark of night no longer feared,
where only lightness is revered.
Instead my sight is compromised,
blurred, distorted often blind,
unlike the promise your's can't hide,
wisdom, patience, forgiving, kind.

I simply wish your eyes were mine.

How close were we

How close were we?

When she was cut I bled,
her heart beat so stong
mine followed her rhythm
Her pain, nor her joy
were hers alone
as everything,
they were shared.
Her smile was my happiness
her tears wreaked havoc on my soul

She was near me,
on me,
in me
every part of me
wanted every part of her
to walk away was suicide
to stay,
a sometimes harder stride.

She'll never leave my memory
The love that's lost,
forever grieved
I can't forget
how close were we

Whole Again

I often wonder;
the path to get back to feeling whole?
What does that look like?
Can I get back to feeling whole?
Will I ever feel whole again?
Doubtlessly there will always be a piece of me missing,
That belongs to her.
There will always be a hole in my heart,
And when my wayward mind drifts
And my shattered soul aches
There remains a small reservoir of loss
Pooled behind my eyes
Waiting to retrace the tracks
That have been laid
By the tears already shed

Shared

I don't think that I was ever
Completely open and honest before
That I ever shared all I had to share with someone
She was the only person I could do that with
I rue my time away from her
The emptiness is unyielding
It's crushing to lose that rare,
Unique closeness with
Someone who I felt safe enough,
Trusted enough to be vulnerable

A Long Road Ahead

The road to healing is long,
Fraught with dangerous twists and turns
At times, insurmountable,
A constant uphill battle
Getting to the destination
Will take time
Especially since she took the Mercedes
And left me with the scooter

Farther

Every once in awhile I brave the day,
Gaze out in the distance
To see a flash of light
Stretch across the horizon
Like a ray of promise
A band of hope inches higher
Cresting the barren desert
Of broken hearts

My weary pulse surges
My lungs regain the air
My eyes react wide open
Into Chance and promise
I must stare

It is then that I realize
I'm thinking of her again
I have to keep them open
To fight against the burning dryness
Focus on the light
Strain to hold that feeling
And savor the taste
Of each sweet, succulent memory
Just
A while
Longer

For I know
That if I blink
It will surely pass
And the cooling,
Soothing of tears will come
And wash her farther away

Stages

The stages of grief?
What are they?
Denial, anger, forgiveness,
I'm not even sure
And it doesn't matter anyway
I don't care
I've tried them all
What I do know is that in my grief
I can go through all of the stages
And still miss her

Medicine

Sometimes I'm lonely
A heart grown cold
A soul so alone
Sometimes it's only
With thoughts untold
That I reach out for her medicine

Relief

I guess that there is some measure of relief
Knowing that I won't be falling short in meeting
Someone else's expectations
With failure again

Shattered

Shattered, nearly broken
Held on desolations edge,
Desperately clinging, hoping,
Hanging by a thread,
Shattered, nearly Broken
Unequivocally unfed,
Future left unspoken
Wreaked emptiness instead

The Chauffeur

She was the most beautiful Chauffeur
I had ever seen.
She really knew how
To handle a Car.
And boy,
Did she take me for a ride

My Fix

She kept me high
On her touch
Buzzed in her presence
And stoned on hope and promise
Her words were wet with closeness
Her eyes said the unspoken
Desire raged unbroken

Kept me guessing
On the run
Out of balance,
Overcome
Until finally
It was said and done

In the aftermath I'm fiending
I'm left empty and I'm needing
Got all these nervous ticks
I'm jonesing for my fix

Yes, the party was awesome
But coming down, crashing to the ground
And detoxing is numbing

Except

Trust is seldom valued
Except by those who cheat
Love is rarely measured
Except by those who leave
Truth is hardly questioned
Except by those who lie
Pain is not forgotten
Except by those who die

Perhaps

I've always thought of myself
as a hopeless romantic
Perhaps what I've done
Is hopelessly romanticized

Ashes Of Destruction

You can only
Stoke the fires of love
For so long
Before they burn you
Or they burn out
It takes a commitment
To nurture a steady blaze
But then you left
And fames scorched me
With fresh wounds
Over old scars
Now I'm left
Sifting through the mess,
Elbow deep in sizzling embers
Of the memory of what was
And the dirty ash of destruction

Enough

Some people measure enough
In tender moments
In soft, sweet kisses
In Comfortability
Some people measure enough
In attentiveness
In affirmation, words of love
In vulnerability
Some people measure enough
In raw attraction
In unbridled passion
In the throes of Pleasure
Some people measure enough
In the sum of money
In the safe of security
In dollars and 'sense'

What I now measure in enough
Is that I wasn't

Expectations

When one person
places their expectations on another
they are setting themselves up for disappointment
and the other person for failure.
I failed, I didn't live up
to the expectation she had of me.
I'm sad and sorry that I couldn't
Meet her vision
But In truth, I'm okay with me
I only expect to do my best
I think I'm kind, caring, honest, loving,
Supportive, truthful, patient and understanding;
For the most part
I wish I could've been enough
For the ending would've been far better
If it were happy
But then again
Maybe she is not fooling herself
And she is happy

The Answer

I'm neither looking for
nor offering any answers in these words.

They are simply a form of therapy,
an outlet of sorts.

To find the real answers one must only
kneel and look up!

Afterword

The aftermath of a true romance unrealized can be tragic and difficult.

We'll always wonder about what could've been, if circumstances had been different, what we might've changed. When something feels so right we'll always question what went wrong, we're human, it's intrinsic to our nature. We are compelled to do our 'emotional forensics', to sift through the debris of a broken heart and examine the clues, gather the shattered remains and try to piece together the 'crime scene'. Unfortunately, that need often comes with lingering emotions, hampering any separation process. It can be exhausting.

I've been told to expect a month for every year together to 'get over' a past love. That is absurd. You can't quantify emotional bonds. Every person and every relationship is different. There is no clear cut, simple formula for healing. One simply wakes up, breathes, places one foot in front of the other and keeps moving forward until slowly, the clouds begin to clear and the light starts to shine again.

Intense romances are even far more strenuous on the psyche and soul. These can weigh heavily on a person for years.

Of course it is my hope that any words that have been penned within might somehow resonate with anyone who is going through or has experienced that extreme pain of the cataclysmic detachment from a true love.

That kind of deep, unyielding hurt, it seems, can only be washed away by the repeated traces of tears, the hearts own cleansing elixir.

2nd afterward

We loved intensely for a long time. she loves sex and for awhile, she loved it with me. She says she can do without it, it's not a necessary thing but she's fooling herself. There has never been a more passionate woman, a more sensuous lover. The ride was exciting, steamy, euphoric and crushing but an incredible experience. To read the entire story

From end to end,
The entire journey,
The Good the bad and the in between
Look for the next book entitled

The last spark

Acknowledgement

Love can truly be so grand but it can also open the door to heartbreak.

Without having experienced the greatest love of my life I might never have come to a place where this kind of writing poured out of me. I had never tried it before but it was as if the floodgates opened in an instant. It came so fast that it dripped through my fingers as I tried to capture the love she ignited, reconcile the feelings of despair that washed through me when we separated and the hope that returned with her, onto paper. So, I would have to thank her first, the catalyst for this effort, she who took me from the highest of highs to the bottom of the abyss and back again.

Am I better for the journey? Only time will tell.

How do you thank everyone who has your back, supports you, helps keep you focused or moving forward?

With my deepest appreciation: My dearly departed mom without her encouragement I'd never have even tried, Her – my dream, My kids and immediate family, Oscar & Amber, Michelle, Cousin Lisa, Scott, Aunt Gaye, Aunt Bonnie, Cheryl, Raz and Pops to whom I owe so much, Shirley, Anita, Teresa, Geoff & Rita and of course anybody else I cornered with the story of this amazing love.

About the author

Guitarist, singer/songwriter, artist, photographer and fledgling author; Sean enjoys living in the creative space.

Made in the USA
Middletown, DE
26 August 2022